Cicero Willis Harris

A Glance at Government

Short Essays on the Rise and Basis of Government

Cicero Willis Harris

A Glance at Government
Short Essays on the Rise and Basis of Government

ISBN/EAN: 9783337133313

Printed in Europe, USA, Canada, Australia, Japan

Cover: Foto ©ninafisch / pixelio.de

More available books at **www.hansebooks.com**

A GLANCE AT GOVERNMENT

SHORT ESSAYS ON

*THE RISE AND BASIS OF GOVERNMENT,
THE STUDY OF POLITICS, THE UNITY
OF SOVEREIGNTY, AND THE
SAVING PRINCIPLE*

BY

CICERO W. HARRIS

AUTHOR OF "A (FORTHCOMING) HISTORY OF THE
SECTIONAL STRUGGLE"

PHILADELPHIA
PRINTED BY J. B. LIPPINCOTT COMPANY
1896

THIS LITTLE BOOK IS DEDICATED, WITH THE

PROFOUND RESPECT OF THE AUTHOR,

TO HIS FRIEND

B. J. SAGE, Esq.,

AUTHOR OF " THE REPUBLIC OF REPUBLICS,"

SINCEREST OF AMERICAN POLITICAL THINKERS.

PREFACE.

THE first two divisions of this "Fragment of Government"* treat of government in general; the last three, of government in the United States. The whole is simply what its title imports,—"A Glance at Government."

CICERO W. HARRIS.

WASHINGTON, February, 1896.

* Bentham.

CONTENTS.

7

THE

RISE OF GOVERNMENT.

No statement of the origin of civilization and government is reasonable which does not take into consideration the condition of the world as it is revealed by research into prehistoric manners and customs. In other words, the world of to-day is not the world of yesterday in important particulars. Sir John Lubbock, with the instinct of the naturalist, seeks in the present life and usages among savages the key to the mysteries of the archaic past. He thinks he finds in the endogamy and exogamy of the Polynesians and Southern Africans, in the brute-like solitude of the Dyaks of Borneo, and in various other traits of barbarous peoples in the existing world a sufficient explanation of what lay beyond the ken of the oldest students in the early ages of

India, Persia, Egypt, Greece, Etruria, and "almighty Rome." On the other hand, such historical investigators into law and government as Sir Henry Maine, men of supreme fidelity to the critical method and of comprehensive and luminous intellects, have not availed themselves of all the knowledge within their reach,—knowledge which would have modified their views on some topics and extended their outlook in all directions. Perhaps, after all, the truest view of the origin of civilization has been taken by those French and German scientists who are free from scepticism, on the one hand, and from the transcendental notions of modern philosophy on the other. The critical method has ascertained during this century at least these cardinal points bearing on our subject: The true philology, without which any study of early institutions would be impossible; through that the foundation of Aryan civilization in the wonderful Sanscrit texts; the knowledge of early Roman law in the discovery by Niebuhr at Rome of the treatise by the great jurisconsult, Gaius;

the "finds" in Behistun, Nineveh, Rosetta, and on the upper Nile, the revelations (vague as they are) of the Moabitish mountain cities, the very latest unearthings of Troy, Tiryns, and Mykænæ by Schliemann. The age has been prolific of the most brilliant and the most profound scholarship. To mention the mere names of the investigators would take the space of an article of more than average length, and then—such is human infirmity—some of the very greatest would inevitably be omitted.

Early man,—what was he, absolutely and relatively? Far down in the bowels of Southwestern France, in ancient Germany, in the kitchen-middens of Denmark, in the mounds of North America, remains of an extinct civilization have recently been exhumed. With the buried races of Neanderthal and Cro-Magnon, at least, savans have remarked the presence of the implements of civilization far different from any known to exist among the races of man which have flourished in the geological period in which we live. Crude but distinct drawings on bone far in advance of the execution of the lowest savages of our age have been recovered. It has been seen that the polar bear, the mammoth, the reindeer of a huge now non-existent species, stalked the plains and primeval forests of Gaul and the Netherlands. Trees that no longer live in such latitudes have been found in the peat bogs of Scandinavia. Philology has come to the aid of palæontology and archæology, and words have been unravelled and roots have been traced through a dozen languages up to their primitive source or sources. Instead of the verbal culture which simplified the speech of early man, as heretofore imagined, we see that he spoke in polysyllables words of learned length and thundering sound. Indeed, all of our forefathers' ideas with respect to primitive culture have been revolutionized. Science has blown its breath on them, and they have perished.

The first man was timorous. He trembled, as Montesquieu says, at the fall of a leaf. But when other men came, and

association was formed, we had the first
society. It came about in mutual need
and knowledge. Men, like some animals,
must have company. The first movement
was probably friendly, the second hostile ;
some men, not satisfied with what they had
by occupation or combination, made war
for conquest or imagined self-protection on
others. Hence associations for government and wars of conquest and aggran-
dizement.

Before diversity of race arose there was
civilization and government. Before nations there were tribes. Before tribes
there were communities. Before communities there were families. The first
governor of men was the patriarch, the
first rule that of *patria potestas,* as the
civil lawyers phrase it. Out of the need
of society sprang the rule of the one.
But it was not perhaps in the beginning a
despotic rule, as of an absolute master
over life and property, but representative,
the father first, then the father's direct de-
scendants, then his fictitious representa-
tives, and last of all a collateral descend-

ant. The patriarch among Chaldeans,
Hebrews, and Hindoos was head of the
family in religious usage as well as
material concerns. He offered the earliest
sacrifices as pontifex maximus by right of
his position. The very earliest worship
was that of a Supreme Being—it may
have been anthropomorphic or otherwise.
The Hebrew and Semitic God was a per-
sonal deity. But the Aryan Dyaus-pitar
(Heaven-father) seems to have been a
Divine Reason embodied, if embodied, in
the grand element that was imminent in
thought and potency at the moment. If
lightning, it was Indra ; if earthly creature,
Agni ; and so forth. The earliest religious
culture was simple but very pure. Error
crept in apace as wealth was acquired and
the conquering arms brought under newer
and lower races. It is not necessary to
accept all the philosophers say as to the
origin of religion. Suffice it to claim as
probably true that all races, all nations
that have appeared on the earth, have
been worshippers in some guise of super-
natural power. Among most of the an-

cients this power or these powers were a part of the visible world or universe. The modern notion of abstraction of deity seems to have been but dimly grasped by a few of the more elevated minds among the ancients. In India, religion continued to be the basis of society and government. The Brahmans superseded the Vedic hymnologists, and laid heavy burdens on the conscience. At first there was no caste. Then the Brahman claimed an intellectual and spiritual primacy. He did not arrogate material pomp and dignity, but left, as a general thing, the administration of the regal government to the two other high-caste elements, the Kshatriya and Vaisyha. But he was priest, lawyer, and teacher. Failing other heirs, and sometimes even if there were other heirs, he succeeded to his pupils' estate.

The world was probably peopled from Armenia or the table-lands of Pamir, in the northwest of India and northeast of Afghanistan, south of Central Asia.* But

---

* Latham gives Germany as the birthplace of the Aryan nations.

there is respectable authority among phil-
ologists and ethnologists for the statement
that the original home of the Aryan or
Indo-European family of nations was in
Germany.   Geiger quotes on this head
the Englishman Latham with entire ap-
probation, but without any convincing
argument.   It is certain that only a small
part of the great human species belongs
to this progressive race.   The larger portion springs from other sources, and has
remained, if not stationary, at least at a
comparatively low state of development
within the knowledge of civilized peoples.
But it is a mistake to rate such races as
the Finns, the Arabs, the Chinese, as un-
deserving of the notice of historians and
anthropologists.   Possibly the theory of
the Frenchman Quatrefages, a very con-
servative investigator, is the correct one:
they arrived at a period of development
commensurate with their physical and
mental powers, and while their skulls in-
dicate the ability to make enlargement of
faculties, the disposition has been wanting,
due probably, as another authority states,

to the morbid character of their ancestor worship. However that may be, and we know that religion is one of the most important bases of national character,—however, we say, that may be, the master race of history has been the Aryan, taking any considerable stretch of time in which to judge. But, as might easily be shown, it is not the great Aryan race which first built cities and established empires, which founded the science of astronomy, which invented letters ; but that people of lingual affinity with the Turks and Finns, the Accadians, or ancient Chaldeans.* Both Assyria and Egypt were probably in existence before the earliest invasion of what is now known as Hindostan. The Aryans were first a hunting then a pastoral race, long before they knew what commerce was or had a name for ship or ocean.

We have not discussed the unity or variety of mankind, but have rather as-

---

* The very latest investigators seem to throw some doubt on this, but I have kept the text unaltered as indicating the probable view.

sumed the former. It is a demonstrable theory, aside from Scriptural revelation. But space is wanting for proofs. Some of the more recent scientists have shown that both Darwin and Agassiz were mistaken in the assumption of various origins of the human species.

In this essay the physical method has been relied upon in part and the lingual in part; for science is one, and the basis of civilization is neither exclusively mental nor entirely moral, however much the ethical and philosophical elements may enter into the statement.

Before defining what we mean by government and liberty, let us sum up the particulars of elementary man. 1. We have a creature at the head of creation, endowed with reason and free agency. 2. His relations are with, first, a supreme Creator and Governor; second, his fellowmen; third, his own future. These relations determine his whole status and fix him in the scale of being. They are necessary to his continued rational existence. Without the idea of God he is

spiritually hopeless. Without civil relations he is a cave-dweller, adrift on the
wilderness, at the mercy of the strongest
and fiercest, having no comfort, no real
pleasures, no mental exhilaration, no def-
inite aims of existence, no care for anything higher or better than simple food,
scant raiment, crude lodging, and content
with these and physical safety from the
storm and ravening beast or insidious rep-
tile. Whatever man may have been in the
beginning, he had desires above these, we
believe on evidence : he was endowed with
at least gesture if not simple speech, and he
looked beyond the present life, it may have
been faintly, gropingly, imagining death an
extended sleep with dreams of things he
knew in the life of the present. We conceive of primitive man as a rational creature, and as such possessed of faculties
above those of mere imitation and brute
necessity. We conceive of him as a moral
creature, recognizing God through that
spark from the Divine Spirit, his immortal
soul. We conceive of him, last of all, as
a social being compelled by the instincts

and aspirations of his order to make society and established government for his own welfare and pleasure.

The first government was patriarchal. As the wants of men and the number of men increased families became village communities or septs, and these in turn formed by association, clans, tribes, and nations. At first, all of the members of the little state were bound by close con-sanguineous ties. Then, as the common-wealth grew, the family (this was in India, but something like it was seen in other early nations) became a sort of fiction and was incorporated by the name of Joint Undivided Family. The *patria potestas* was extended to the nearest of kin in the direct line, presently to be supplied in de-fault of heirs by various substitutes and the collateral kindred. The principle of representation is not once lost, but is kept alive even after the joint family has passed (not by absorption, however) into the tribe and the father or father's representative has become the chieftain. In this primi-tive state, some of the philosophers and savans represent, the wives as well as the lands and flocks were communal. Religion in the far East, at least, degenerated into ancestor worship or the cult of the pitris. The more Eastern nations reached early a stage of considerable cultivation and stopped developing, perhaps not suddenly, perhaps not altogether at all, but only by comparison with the Western robust nations of modern times. The highest culture ever obtained was that of Athens, the highest jurisprudence that of Rome. There is nothing in the art and law of India and China comparable with the ideas of the Periclean, Augustan, and Justinian ages.

This essay is too short for a review of the influence of religion and culture upon law and government. We know that some nations who achieved a noble development in art and literature had low ideals in religion and defective principles of government. But it is probably safe to say that no permanent and high civilization in the completest sense is possible where there is no just conception of the relation between these branches of civilization. Certainly the remark is true of some ancient nations whose civilization is buried and lost. Egyptian beast and river worship, the external form of an internal religion,—that of the priests,—may not at first glance consort with the grand, massive art of Luxor and the splendors of Memphis. But the servile people, who obeyed their own natures in bowing down to the crocodile and the will of a tyrant in placing great stones one upon the other, through centuries, fell at last into such degradation as has overtaken only those nations who have imitated their example or, without having it before their eyes, have adopted its spirit. The high Aryan conqueror, springing from the cradle of nations and waving his scimitar as his warrant of authority, may not in the earlier days of his power have had "the wisdom of the Egyptians," but he had what was far better, a clearer idea of his place among men and his responsibility to the Supernal Power.

Man is great by inheritance and effort. The German, Celtic, and Slavonian races are the foremost because they have not

sold their birthright for a mess of pottage.
Not the first to leave their ancestral seats
among the high table-lands of Asia, back-
ward it may be said in building empires,
these Indo-Europeans going westward and
southward, never eastward, have hewn out
at last a gigantic civilization of ideas and
freedom which is fast overspreading the
earth with its power and beneficence.   It
has been fashionable to obscure the religious side of our Aryan ancestors, and
to speak of those ideas as coming altogether from an alien and inferior race, the
Semitic.   Not so do we read the book of
their history as seen in the study of lan-
guage, in the remains of rude art and in
the fragments of Greek, Roman, and Hin-
doo literature, to say nothing of tradition,
folk lore, existing laws, customs, and manners.   Max Müller's translations have
made the present generation familiar with
the religion of the first Hindoos.   It was
not a crude pagan worship of stocks,
stones, and reptiles, but the adoration of
the grand powers of Nature as typifying
the One Power ineffable in heaven far

away. Let us never lose sight of this great
fact. The gods of Northman and Teu-
ton, although harsher in their vindictive
aspect than Aditi and the seven supreme
gods of the Vedas, were not the fierce
spirits of darkness to propitiate whose ma-
lign power the Shaman prays and shakes
his rattle. No god of Kaffir or Australian
in our advanced age rivals Balder. What
a distance in conception of human and
divine relations is there between the Poly-
nesian and the most primitive Aryan!

We reach another stage of thought here.
Has civilization always progressed, or has
it sometimes receded through ages in
certain nations and races? This is the
philosopher's crux. We hold, against a
powerful school, that there has not been
uniform, nor anything approaching uniform,
progression, as there has certainly not been
uniform retrogression. The world is wiser
in the extent of its information, prouder
in the grandeur of its aims, purer in the
increasing beneficence of its institutions;
the world is richer in mental, moral, and
material means to the ends of a just and

ideal civilization. Progress has been gradual, steady, nearly uniform, but there have been great wastes where scarce an oasis was to be discerned by the solitary investigator. It will not do to say that these were periods of real recuperation hidden behind the appearance of devastation and decay, for that is merely begging the question, which is one of absolute and not comparative decadence. The fall of Carthage and the long subsequent dissolution of Roman dominion left all North Africa in a state of semi-barbarism, from which even the sway of the enlightened Saracen did not relieve it. No successor arose to this Saracen in his original home, and to this day the seats of the Arabians, the Syrians, the Assyrians' empire, are occupied by the detested and degenerate Turk. Nothing can be alleged of the fall of the Romans in their eternal city and the countries of its conquests, because the civilization of the Romans, plus the mental, moral, and other characteristics of the Goths, forms the grandest type of racial and national character the world has ever recognized.

BASIS OF GOVERNMENT.

WHAT is government? what rational
liberty?

On the answers to these questions de-
pend the happiness and welfare of any
people. Should we say with the learned
and eloquent author of the "Spirit of
Laws," that that is the best government
which best suits the genius of a people
and which is also the best administered?
Or, with more modern ideas, borrowed
probably from some of the Greeks, must
we hold that that government is the model
which is most consonant with popular desires? After all, the view of Montesquieu
and the view of the republican are not in-
compatible. The people, sooner or later,
will adopt a democratic government if not
restrained or kept in a state of gross ignorance and servility. Restraints are un-

26

successful after a people have had a glimpse of liberty. Now let us not be hidebound. There is liberty under other forms of government than the republican. Some constitutional monarchies are monarchies only in name. Some republics have been very despotisms for at least short periods. Athens was under Cleon. Rome, under Scylla, was a confessed tyranny. The present governments of England and Sweden-Norway are very liberal, and, if there were no friction between church and state, Italy would be regarded almost universally as a model of a state having free institutions. In fact, the tendency of modern thought has been steadily to freedom, with occasional lapses· for short periods and notable exceptions for longer ones. The free Gothic spirit of old Spain is again breaking forth in the " Ever Faithful Isle," and Teutonic liberty in Fatherland has not always slept since the days of Hermann, and is not now slumbering.

On the setting up of our experiment, it was seen that ideals of statesmen and philosophers were possible of realization.

Indeed, no ideal had ever been formed quite equal to the state of facts exhibited in the United States. Whether we borrowed of the Greek or the Italian republics, of the United Netherlands, of Switzerland, of the Hanseatic League, of Rousseau's conception of a Social Compact, or fused all these with existing remains of our colonial dependency,—the models we took from Britain,—the result was something unique and world-pervading. This is no place in which to consider separate models of government or deal philosophically with government in the abstract. We certainly cling to no threefold division of governments, such as those of Tacitus and Montesquieu, usually adopted by writers. To us it suffices that governments seem to be as to their spirit free and despotic, with shades between. May we not be permitted to state compendiously that all enlightened government is either democratic or aristocratic, seeing that in absolute monarchies on the modern plan the noble class, or a part of it, controls the sovereign as an *imperium in imperio?*

The great fact in government is the
administration. As the people in liberal
governments appreciate this fact, there will
be improvement in their condition. All
through history we see the law of action
and reaction between rulers and ruled.
At last we have reached the period of full
representation which precludes the use of
such words: the people rule themselves,
—in theory, at least.

This is a most wonderful step forward.
The brilliant Athenian thought he had
taken it when his Eupatrid order ceased
to control the affairs of state. But, alas!
he legislated merely for the day: impatient
to grasp everything at once, he did not lay
very deep and secure the foundations of
social order and popular freedom. The
Italian republics, modelled on those of an-
tiquity, and adapted to the purposes of
mediæval trade, fell far short of perfection.
Faction became the curse of all, and on
the ruins of democracy arose a number of
ducal and princely houses. The law of
liberty has been the law of progress, but,
as in culture and civilization generally,

there have not been wanting evidences of
sad decline. We take heart from what we
see and feel about us in contrast with what
we know is behind. Whether government,
as has been insisted by Rousseau and
Jefferson, is based altogether in its original
on contract or consent, or, as held by
writers of the adverse school, on power, is
neither worth our while to consider as a
practical question nor to reject altogether
as having no interest for the political stu-
dent. What we know is that at some
stage in human development the idea of
consent was adopted. It is our basis now,
possibly by slow evolution, with occasional
set backs, from a primitive state in which
the patriarch ruled his family, son, and
servant, with a measure of absolute authority as the representative head. In the
second stage we have the principle of
representation carried further: the nearest kinsman rules. The third stage brings
on the elected chieftain. Always there is
progress from power to liberty.

Is this view less flattering to human
vanity or less tenable upon investigation

than that in which man now recovers what
was his in the beginning without limitation,
but which he through weakness yielded?
Is all our safety in revolution, and is there
no security in the essential dignity of human nature and in the flexible but un-
erring law of progress?

THE

STUDY OF POLITICS.

IN these days, when "Confound your politics" is a popular refrain, it is fitting that the study of government should be carried on more scientifically than at any previous era of the world's history. And yet there is great danger that what is gained in knowledge of details and nicety of methods may be lost in accuracy of scholarship and comprehensiveness of principles. As science itself becomes a matter of specialization very largely, so political science, a segment of the circle, is apt to become unduly specialized. It can afford, least of all sciences, to submit to this narrowing process. Taught in school and college, without recourse to the elemental principles of human nature and too much as a thing apart, with only

32

slight reference to the fundamental ordinary facts of life, and devoid frequently of those illustrations drawn from the parliamentary annals and the originals of history, it is the mere husk of information, a showy sham and mocking pretence. As to those parts of comparative politics bearing directly on representative institutions and the development of republican government, we have plenty of learned disquisition on the classic states, the mediæval republics, and on the concrete idea of the state itself,—the modern state, with its autonomous functions and international obligations. But of the reason of being of our own particular form of government, as shown by the facts of its formation and preservation, the teaching of the day is absurdly meagre and strangely misleading. The vast wealth of historical accumulation mined within the past four or five decades should have made this otherwise. The great stores of information brought forth by German and English and American antiquarians and historians ought long since to have been absorbed

into the popular manuals, and thus gone
into general knowledge. The fact is that
as to the fundamental features of our own
institutions the early generations were
better informed, except as to a very few
things, than the later; there has been distinct and woful degeneracy on a matter
of vital consequence to American citizen-
ship. Whether, when all the passions of
a period of feverish national unrest shall
have subsided, the political ground lost
shall have been recovered in time to pre-
vent grave detriment to our society, cannot be predicted, but the fear of some
wise men is that even the salvation of the
union is not itself, great a fact as it is by
all admitted to be, sufficient recompense
for the retrogradation in the essential here
described. No people ought ever to for-
get its organic character, even for a short
period. Perhaps no people ever do entirely. And this doubt that it does relieves
the philosophic mind from much of the
uncertainty on this head.

The study of institutions is the pro-
foundest and most engaging of all secular

studies. It is of wider human interest than any other, and has most of all to do with human affairs, so far as they shape themselves with reference to merely transitory ends. And even in the contemplation of the permanent order that exists for us beyond the present life, the science of government is of transcendent utility and surpassing fascination. At least, it is so for all broadly-based intellects. There is only the shadow of a truth in the pessimistic remark of Thomas Paine that "government is a necessary evil." We must recognize the sharp limitations of human virtue, and thus see that restraint is a part of the economy of existence. Therefore government is a necessary good, not evil. The evil in society is the evil in each human being, plus the evil in humanity, minus the good in each human being, plus the good in humanity. The study of politics, therefore, is the study of the best good for society, and if it result otherwise, it is because the end is perverted, and not because it is not a true end.

This leads to my formula: Politics is

the application of the good that is possible to the existing status. This formula does not exclude ideals. Ideals become reals when the conditions for reality exist. The philosopher cherishes ideals, the statesman adapts them to circumstances. The ideal is Goethe's "ever-womanly," drawing us on to infinite heights after almost infinite suffering. The great tragedy of "Faust" is life's tragedy with a miracle at the beginning and at the end.

Human government is the most complex of humanly-created things. It demands for its exercise the best powers of the human character. The government of the United States is the most complex of all governments in history. Its safety consists in its being always what it was intended to be by those who formed it— a government of the peoples of the several States, forming what Washington and Franklin, Hamilton and Madison, Jay and Jefferson styled in the well accepted phrase of their day "a confederacy." With the spirit of representative democracy and the form of a confederated republic, its name describing itself better than any formal description could, the republic of the United States stands as the heir of Teutonic primæval institutions and the free spirit of the Aryan race in all its branches.

4

THE

UNITY OF SOVEREIGNTY.

SOVEREIGNTY in a state is that which is over all, governing all. There is no conflict of opinion as to what is sovereign in Great Britain or Russia. The government in each nation is master, absolute and, except as to the claims of Nihilists and other cranks, unchallenged master. These governments differ, and so the sovereign is not the same in both. One is free, the other despotic. But in both instances it is the government, and not the people, who constitute the sovereignty. It is true that, in the former, a large portion of the public is directly interested in choosing the House of Commons, which is the virtual governor of the kingdom, but the sovereignty is vested, after all, in the government, and

38

not, as with us, in the persons who elect the government. The difference, in brief, between the United States and the United Kingdom of Great Britain and Ireland is this:—The republic has never clothed its agents with sovereignty, the monarchy has. Under the unwritten constitution of "Our Old Home" absolute sovereignty vests—no matter whether originally by public consent, as contended for by Freeman the historian, or not—in the House of Commons, which uses fictions implying sovereignty in the King or Queen. The Parliament has gradually acquired sovereignty, and the House of Commons has more and more acquired single control over everything. The cabinet comes and goes as the House changes its will. The nominal sovereign still addresses her "Lords and Gentlemen," but in truth they, or rather the latter, are her masters.

The people of the United States retained sovereignty in the beginning. They could not part with it without loss of autonomy. They cannot part with it now without such loss. All the writers on public law affirm

the truth of this philosophical negative.
It is, in fact, self-evident.

If, as has been defined, sovereignty is
that which is over all, which governs or
controls all in an unqualified sense, we
may easily see that while the King in an
absolute monarchy, the King and legislature in some, and the legislature with "the
government" in other constitutional monarchies is sovereign, the people only in a
republic are sovereign.   Therefore, here
the people of the United States possess
the sovereignty.   A fallacious idea has
occasionally been expressed, that the Constitution of the Union is the sovereign.
That could not be because it is the simple
expression of the will of the true sovereigns
on certain points.   At other times the fallacy
has even been more ludicrous, namely, that
each individual, suffrage-endowed citizen
is a sovereign, and that there are as many
sovereigns in the United States as there
are citizens entitled to vote.   This refutes
itself, because these citizens are such by the
will of the State.   Again, the exigencies of
argument have driven many late writers

on public law to declare without reason, except the physical one of a restored Union after a bloody war, that the people of the United States are one people,—whether at the Declaration of Independence or the adoption of the present Constitution they do not agree. The old State rights school still holds to the sovereignty of the States as States, and not in a confederacy.*

---

* "Confederacy" is the word used by Washington, Madison, Hamilton, and others among the founders of the government.

Right here I will observe that even the wise old fathers did not always carry in their minds the distinction between the sovereign State and the legislature of a State,—a distinction sometimes lost sight of completely in more recent times. The sovereignty of a State resides only in its people. It is expressed in its final absolute form in the State's adoption of an organic law either for itself or the confederation of which it is a part.

Mr. Hurd's concept of a Union-State always sovereign, with power to coerce North Carolina and Rhode Island when they chose for a time to remain out of the Union of States under the new Constitution, is not historical, whatever else it is. It is not in line with the facts he uses so powerfully to demolish the arguments of the consolidation school.

The great writers concur with Vattel,* who says, " every sovereignty, properly so called, is, in its own nature, one and indivisible." Montesquieu, Locke, Puffendorf, Burlamaqui, Liebig, and others, all speak of the indivisibility of sovereignty.

The mistake has arisen either from the necessity for making it or honestly from a confusion of ideas. It is not remembered that the sovereign is the possessor, and the powers are the things possessed. The old theory of our federal government was that it was a simple agency of the people of the several States. It would seem that few in strictness hold that theory now. And yet there would appear to be no reason for abandoning it in view of the history of the two constitutions the country has lived under. If, as the Supreme

---

Discussions as to the fundamental character of our government are always in order, and, while I make no apology for adhering to the State rights school, I utterly disclaim any purpose to unsettle anything which may ever have been definitively settled.

* Book I., Sec. 65, cited by Sage, " Republic of Republics," p. 306, Fifth edition.

Court of the United States held in the slaughter-house cases, there has been no fundamental changes in the structure of our government as a result of the Civil War, there is nothing to induce the thoughtful citizen to alter or modify the former view of the nature of our institutions,—the view of the Federalists as well as of the Republicans, of Hamilton as well as of Madison.* After all, there is not much danger that the holding of such

---

* The second of the Articles of Confederation and Perpetual Union between the States declares that "each State retains its sovereignty, freedom, and independence, and every power, jurisdiction, and right, which is not by this Confederation expressly delegated to the United States, in Congress assembled." Here is a precise delimitation, clearly showing the distinction between sovereignty and powers. Hon. John Randolph Tucker, a professor of law in Washington and Lee University, and one of the ablest constitutional lawyers of this generation, tells me that he illustrates the matter thus: Sovereignty is the dynamo; powers are its capabilities.

Nothing that occurred in the formation, adoption, and ratification of the present Constitution, with its various amendments, has in the slightest degree interfered with the distinction drawn in the above Article II.

opinions will break up the confederacy. The tendency of holding it would rather be to cement it. And an honest view, any way, one consonant with the facts, is infinitely preferable to a dishonest one.

THE

SAVING PRINCIPLE.

-

A civic virtue unspotted and unsleeping; a citizenhood both conserving and progressive; a respect everywhere for private rights, and a sense in all breasts of the dignity of human nature and the reflected dignity of human government in a free land; then, as the inevitable result of domestic integrity, a policy of justice *to* foreign powers and of insistence upon justice *from* them, a clear adherence to the American doctrine that America yields nothing to pressure from without and herself exerts no pressure to secure purposes external to her true and traditional policy. These are the moral forces of a great people separated by two oceans from most other powers of the earth and by spirit and structure of government from nearly every one of them.

With a keen eye to home interests, with thorough education for the masses supplanting half-ideas,—a foe infinitely worse, if permanent, than meek ignorance,—with a profound respect for law so long as it is law, and an intelligent choice of lawmakers and administrators, the civic virtue above described is bound to remain forever as the characteristic of the highest development of the greatest race in the world's history. As it has lived in Norway and Switzerland and Great Britain from early times, so it will endure in this younger branch of a great family,—its saving principle.

www.ingramcontent.com/pod-product-compliance
Lightning Source LLC
Chambersburg PA
CBHW022203020726
47496CB00008B/2861